Livestock Man

ISBN: 978-1-68313-156-4
Library of Congress Control Number: 2018942147

Pen-L Publishing
Fayetteville, Arkansas
www.Pen-L.com

First Edition
Printed and bound in the USA

Cover photo by Jessica Brandi Lifland
Dedication photo courtesy of Skip Shumpes
Cover design by Kelsey Rice

Livestock Man

by

Amy Hale Auker

poems from a rebel heart

Books by Amy Hale Auker

Essays:

Rightful Place

Ordinary Skin: Essays from Willow Springs

Novels:

Winter of Beauty

The Story Is the Thing

Poetry:

Livestock Man

To my father, Tom Hale. I wish I knew calligraphy.

Contents

Introduction: Meeting Silas

The Christmas I was eight years old I unwrapped a *Webster's New World Dictionary of the American Language*. My father's hand-written inscription read:

To Amy
From Mama and Daddy, Christmas 1978
May you always be as eager to learn,
As quick to laugh,
As easy to love,
As you have always been.
God bless you.

I came to poetry sideways, like a sailboat beating into the wind. I was raised by livestock men who loved language and literature. Their shelves were full of books. Their mouths were full of words, even as their hands worked with animals and the land. Even as they built fence, climbed windmills, and shod horses. My father threw out the television when I was five years old. My parents read aloud to us for hours on end. One very hot summer I memorized several poems and recited them with my sister, standing on the cool hearth of an old ranch house. We tasted the words of the poets on our tongues. My father taught high school English for many of those years and I pulled literature anthologies from his shelves, sitting on the floor with those heavy volumes open on my lap. The poetry was tucked amongst the prose. My father read Longfellow to us, *The Village Blacksmith* and *Paul Revere's Ride*. My birthday is April 18, and I thrilled to the line of that poem: "*On the eighteenth of April, in Seventy-Five . . .*"

When I got to high school, I doubled up on math classes my sophomore year, taking both Geometry and Algebra II so as to catch up with an advanced-with-honors degree program. English class rescued me from despair, introduced me to e e cummings and William Carlos Williams, poets unbounded by lines and numbers. I can still see *The Red Wheelbarrow* on the page of our literature text.

The teacher instructed us to imitate Williams's poem *This Is Just To Say*, to write poems of our own that mimicked it in form and parts of speech. As an assignment, it was brilliant. I went overboard. Of course I did. For years I kept those imitations that I wrote on lined notebook paper, though I can't find them now. I also kept a contraband copy of cummings's *may I feel said he*, the sexiest thing I had encountered up to that time. I probably wrote thirty versions of *This Is Just To Say*. I had to choose three to turn in, though I am sure I wanted to turn in the whole sheaf. My poor teacher. I got so carried away with the assignment, and allowed my imagination such freedom, that when I got home, my mother had *that look* on her face. Seems that one of the poems I chose to turn in was the one where I replaced *I have eaten the plums* with *I have lost the baby*. English was my third period class. Sometime after that, during the day, my English teacher had called my mother to make sure that she hadn't miscarried recently. My poor mother.

During my junior year, I wrote my research paper on Robert Frost. I stuck firmly to those of his poems with structure, rhyme, and meter that I could analyze handily. I had learned the lessons of geometry and algebra while forgetting the early childhood magic of language spilling from memory and tongue. I was rescued by my father. He picked up the collection of Frost's poetry and thumbed through to some of the poems I had been skipping over because I couldn't see what made them poems. I will never forget him standing before me and reading . . . no . . . performing, *Out, Out—*. He made himself cry. Then he flipped the pages over and performed *Death of a Hired Man*. He took a poem I didn't understand and lifted it off the page. It became a story. It came alive. And now my father and I were bound by Silas, though I wasn't aware that we are also bound to all who come to know and love Silas and his ability to build a load of hay, how he *bundles every forkful in its place*, and that we are also bound to those few who would even care that Silas *takes it out in bunches like big birds' nests*. Frost binds those who care with his daring and artistry and story. That research paper, long lost, was better because my father lifted the language from the page and into the air, giving me membership into those who care.

For my seventeenth birthday my father gave me the *Collected Works of Robert Frost*. He was studying calligraphy at the time.

To Amy, with love, Mom and Dad

Several years ago, I wrote my dear friend and editor, Andy Wilkinson, "What is poetry?" The dialogue that ensued was necessary. I considered myself an essayist, and later, a novelist. Never a poet. But because the cowboy poetry and music family is inclusive to a fault, I had been invited to perform at several gatherings. Surely if I can write a collection of essays and some novels, I can write a poem. But I was paralyzed, held captive once again by the mathematics and expectations of good poetry. And yet, I had no way to make those judgments. Andy answered me, "A poem is a completed act of poetry."

I first knew poetry as an oral tradition from my father, and now from the cowboy poetry gatherings I had attended and from the hundreds of poems I had heard recited by both master and amateur performers. I knew poetry out loud. For several years, my son Oscar was one of those performers, reciting some of the classic cowboy poets as well as contemporary poets who wrote about a life lived on the land, a life with which he identified. When someone once asked him why he wasn't writing poetry of his own, he said, "I haven't lived long enough to have anything to write about." He was thirteen. Children are our greatest teachers, but their lessons are usually roundabout, rarely in the form of outright statements of truth. But here, for me, was a direct statement. Poetry is experiential. There is no need to reach for something to write about as long as we are living something real. And Andy reinforced that with his own statement that writing should not be done in the moment of passion but during times of *passionate reflection*.

I spend hours and hours of my life on a horse, moving slowly, trailing up cattle or following them for long miles, plodding. I have ample time for passionate reflection. I tell audiences that if I write a poem that rhymes, they can bet I wrote it horseback and needed to remember it when I got home. That isn't necessarily true; I have stored many prose poems in my head as I ride.

A few years later, after having, indeed, written some poetry, I saw Andy at a busy and crowded event. He told me that he was giving a workshop on poetry and songwriting and suggested that I stick my head in. Since I was performing in my own sessions that morning, it was really all I could do . . . stick my head in. But showing up, even in a brief way, has its rewards. I stepped into the back of the room just in time to hear him speak about something he calls the still point, the spark, that magic moment in the creative process when one can see it, can see the possibility, and for just the barest instant, can see it whole, and then it is gone. And then the work commences, though that magic moment hopefully comes around again and again, luring us on. A woman in the audience raised her hand. "When you have that spark, how do you know if it is going to be a poem or a song?" Andy paused. "I don't. It might be a painting." I slipped back out the door.

When my daughter went off to college, another poetic influence began hitting my inbox. Lily discovered slam poets on YouTube. Watching and listening to those poets with strong social consciousness who take the words off the page reminded me of the cowboy poets. Slam poets are irreverent, passionate, and talented, often using the same self-deprecating humor prevalent among agrarian poets. And they make our language sing. They make us pay attention. In this collection, I have included some slam poems about the work that I do. They are best experienced out loud, standing up, moving.

Many of these poems are love stories, love stories to the land, to the past, to the present, to the future, to animals, to tracks in the sand, to hidden seep springs in deep canyons, to witches in the night, to wild grapes and longing, to campfires. But more than anything, they are love stories about work. I did not decide to collect these poems into a volume until recently when I wrote *Letter To My Father, In Three Parts*. That poem, a work poem, I wrote while trotting out into cold wind. It is, indeed, a completed act of poetry.

I can't paint. And I can only sing in front of the fire at night after two whiskies. But my creative process shifted and changed to include this whole new thing. Now, I never know when I begin to write if something is going to be prose or poetry, fiction or non, or a curious mixture of both. I never know when I will be presented with a story that, unless I tell it, will remain untold. I never know when I will meet Silas. And so goes the dance. And so I tack into the wind once again.

A. H. A.

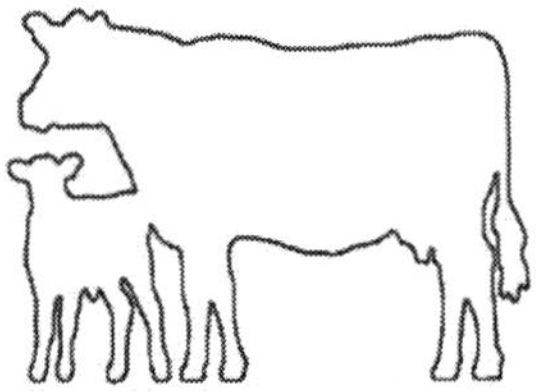

See You at the Barn

See you at the barn
is what you give me
as you turn left
and I turn right
along a ribbon of cedar posts and barbed wire
stretched tight.
Up and down canyons, across ridges,
I make crooked the straight
in deference to equine muscle
and slick rock.

And my brain plays traitor to my heart,
badgers me with
litanies and lists and ledgers,
calendars, costs and clocks,
tick tock.
All those things we have misnamed *real*.
I spur my horse faster.

But this rough ride can't be rushed,
and reality reclaims its right to what is
really real,

and thank God,
I can see again.

Rocks in layers with pebble aprons,
as if they were waterfalls,
and they will be
when the water falls.
Dead trees posed among the living,
as if they were paintings,
and they will be
when the artist brings her brushes.

Bright pink bear scat,
heavy laden with prickly pear seed.
Deer as explosions out of shadows,
rise above me to stand as solid sculptures,
watching.

Tick tock becomes hoof fall and heartbeat,
hoof fall quickening when quinine quivers
with quail whirr,
and my own heart beats when I see
a bright green rattlesnake,
velvet tail, pale buttons,
head flat, coiled tight,
ready to strike,
and he does not buzz.

A hawk is my sailing, silent companion
until he cries, friendlylonely from the air.
A fragile inchworm rests on my sleeve.
Fat green acorns wear tight-knit caps for fall.

Songbirds weave in and out of the
bushes,
and I become one of them
as I weave
with words and with wire.
And so the hours
do not pass,
for I refuse to name them
or claim them as such.
When I turn toward home,
I vow that when I remember,
I will not give time nor day nor task,
but rather, will say,
I remember that moment
when I was alive.

See you at the barn.

Livestock Man

I need to write a new poem about what it is like, as a woman, to cowboy for a living.

But all I can come up with is how much I hate it when my toes get cold.

All I can think about is that last old cow we put on the trailer for the sale barn,
about the scorpion that ran away when I rolled my bed out on the ground
at Alkali Spring in August,
about how I alone can catch that roan mare when she won't let the men lay a hand on her.

All I can come up with is how much I like cows,
and, like them, I have ovulated, copulated, gestated a miracle in my body, and lactated . . .
for months.

I think I'm qualified to be a herder of mammals.

And that is what I am. I am a herder, a custodian, a caretaker, a steward.
I am a livestock man.

I grow food.

I need to write a new poem about what it is like, as a woman, to cowboy.

But there are no new poems and we're never finished shipping cattle in the fall.

There may be new foxes in the night and new orioles in the canyon and new griefs to be
borne and new ways of looking at the world . . .

Oh, please, don't let me become blind.

And I might become blind if you put me in the cage of your expectations.

For I have a rebel heart, and that rebel heart gives me the grit to stay in my saddle even after it turns sideways when the bullfight breaks and we're in the way.

And that rebel heart says this poem . . . doesn't have to rhyme.

I need the language to tell about what it is that I do, but all I have are nouns:

weather and wind and wool,
rock and rattle and remuda.
Smoke and sweat and sunrise and savvy.
Tracks and trails, tinajas and tally.
Cow and count and coffee and canyon,
logistics and latigos and loops.
Moonshadow, mud, mother, manure, moisture in the air.
Hooves and javelina and how sharp is your pocket knife?

I need the words to tell this story but all I have are verbs:

pee in the dirt
and dally up and build again
and don't cry when you get yelled at.
Back off that little heifer and ride up! Don't let that bull bluff you out.
We'll never get him again.
Thaw the frozen coffee pot.
Blink the smoke out of your eyes.
Wipe the blood off your chin.
Dig the snowballs out of your horse's hooves.
Hurry up and get the gate; there's a storm moving in.
Open a can of chili. Let's eat before it gets plumb dark.

I need to write a poem about working for $75 a day,
but all I can think about is that last little cow we left behind up on the mesa.

We'd been gathering into the trap for four days
and our first calf heifers run in the general herd
and our bulls are out year 'round.
She gave birth overnight,

but she didn't bring her newborn in to hay
. . . and we had to go.

We cut her back with that ol' hooky cow's daughter and her calf because that ol' hooky cow's
daughter is mean, meaner than that ol' hooky cow ever thought about being,

. . . and no lion or coyote is going to get that baby.

But then it snowed.

And I don't know what it is you think about when you lie awake at night . . .

Do you ever think of soft tender hooves and fresh new life up under a cedar tree at 6000 feet
with a mama who's new to this gig?

I need to write a new poem about what it is like to cowboy,

without the requisite body parts.

Wanna see my tattoos?

Mediocrity

Fear and scared
needs be locked in a vault of understanding,
like bucked off hard in the rocks.
For we each are the true Frankenstein,
creating our own monsters.
Cavafy calls them Lestrygonians,
reminds us that we carry them with us,
like luggage.
I'll show you mine if I must,
lay you a feast of chainsaws and
electric bread knives
which leads to pressure cookers . . .
kept dusty in corner cabinets.
Kitchen implements, you say?
Things that can get out of control, I counter,
tools that slip and jump over to cut deep.
A ragged bloody mess.
That can blow tops and
splatter scalding pain.
I say silly things like *Let me fly,*
but I don't climb ladders or hang glide—ever.
I am my father's daughter,
Lo, I am with you always.
Proof that God doesn't want us in His sky.
Only understood by the literate, or the Baptists.
Give me a language playground

but keep your joints and pills
and gateway anything,
because I stand free of those cages
until six o'clock when
I pour hypocritical amber . . .
On the rocks,
the cliffs of *I can quit any time.*
I walk the evening tightrope of
It's time to stop trying so hard . . .
because the biggest monster's name
starts with M and ends with being
Good enough
Okay
Decent
Sweet
Pretty
Lukewarm and comfortable
Middle of the road and mainstream.
Thesaurus says
undistinguished and insignificant.
So I climb the highest peak
and hope I grow wings.
Run a chainsaw to stay warm
(ear plugs please)
count my pours of stiff drink,
because I'm no quitter.

Letter to my Father, In Three Parts

Part One

Trotting out
Into cold wind.
Good-looking men,
Fresh horses,
Rough country.
We've had some rain.

Bits of conversation, jokes,
The smoke of roll-your-owns
Drift back my way
Along the trot line.
Time to think
In rhythm,
Before our hands are full
With cows.

And I think of you every time I swing up into the saddle.
Every time we get some rain.

You've left this game.
And some days I understand why.
You were one of those handsome men,
On a fresh horse,
Trotting out.
Perhaps you rolled one of your own,
Blew your smoke and your joke
Into the wind.
You spoke of rain.

Part Two

I was four,
The first time I ever saw you cry.
A heifer stood beneath the windmill,
Dripping blood.
A pack of town dogs
Had chewed her face off.
It was also the first time
I ever saw you load a gun.

Today I reined up,
Let a little red heifer
Drink from the creek,
Before catching up with the rest.
I understood about those town dogs.
But at four,
I didn't realize
The gun was also for the heifer.

Part Three

When the day is hard,
I tell myself to
Tough up.
Your words, Daddy.
I've had worse than that on my eyeball!
But, you would also say,
Everyone does the best he can all the time.

Like you,
I'd quit over a dehorning spoon
Or unnecessary roughness.
Game over.
Like you,
I ride off from the horror.
Like you,
I choose this life of
Wind and work and wild.
Like you,
I understand
Tough up.

Thank you, Daddy.

Teach Me To See

Born blind,
And didn't even know it.
Thought I could see, thought I was,
missed not only the minutiae
but the broad vistas.
I missed the unveiling, the lifting of scales.
I am learning, but slowly.
Teach me to see.

Teach me to see
In the chrysalis, the caterpillar.
In the nymph, the dragonfly.
At the edge of the web, the spider.
Dark sky wings transition at dusk
when the swallow becomes the bat.
Painted canvas hills cradle creeks,
clear with amoeba and skaters.
I see the pinch bug carrying her eggs
until the waterfall wins without trying.
I see the shed skin of a snake
lining the nest of a bird,
lifted from ground, introduced to sky.

Teach me to see
Beyond my nation,
Beyond my appetite.
More than tracks in the dust,
the barefoot bear foot.
To see past the words
or agendas
or ones and zeros
or ancient Jungian bleed.

I see the shadow of his daddy's hands
in his newborn fist.
I see the bruised eyes of love
wrecked on the reef of self,
the closed criticized child,
the laundry list of needing more,
the confusion of colossal change.

Among the boulders and the trees
I begin to see.
Simply. And that is to be.

Wild Grapes on an Ordinary Afternoon

Just an ordinary day until you see them,
Just an ordinary day until you do.
Wild grapes growing high overhead,
Amidst the green, they're dusky blue.

Was an ordinary dawn at the morning,
And with ordinary you filled your cup.
And it would have gone on being ordinary,
Except that you looked up.

The birds usually get them before now.
The birds like to eat them tartly green.
You've been riding all day through ordinary,
Toward this gift, here, at this spring.

So fill your mouth with seedy sweetness,
Fill your hands with purple blue stains.
Your horse, he's content to graze here,
So go on, cowboy, drop the reins.

Let greedy fingers get tangled in the vines,
Let your heart get filled up to the top,
With ordinary magic on this ordinary day,
Because you know how to stop.

You'll ride on from here for many more miles,
And smile at your hands fading to gray.
And you'll think about how paying attention,
Can flip the switch on an ordinary day.

Damn Fine Hands

Roy Rogers, Gene Autry, Rex Allen, Monte Montana, Lone Ranger
got no shit on their boots,
never faced a norther head-on,
or had to lead off the ridge
with loose rocks sliding down the cliff.
Never made a grocery list with a stop at the parts store.
They rode gentle horses.

My father's father raised sheep and goats,
ran a few cows on a Wild Horse River lease.
He spoke Spanish with the shearing crew,
shared their *frijoles* under the mesquite tree.
He was a damn fine hand.

My mother's father poured liquid gold
on alfalfa and cotton out west of town,
skipped Sunday services to wade along the ditches,
hard hands over the ends of black straws,
never failing to set the siphons, one after another.
My father fed four kids nailing iron on rich men's toys,
the smell of hoof shavings embedded in his clothes,
sweat dripping from his nose,
perpetually rough hands
even though he had a teaching degree.

I didn't know the word cowboy.
I knew work.
I knew big ranches and windmills,
fencing tools in the back of the truck.
I knew making a living
and breakfast before dawn in the wet shack.
I knew *chiles* and sale barn saddles and *caliché* dirt.
The men left their spurs on their boots in the saddle house,
never wore their hats inside a building.
They had knives in their pockets, out of sight.

They were damn fine hands.

Too Much Water

Where's the
happy medium
between clinging like a cocklebur
and flitting away like downy fluff, off into the wind?

It's a party scene.
It's a cliché.
It's a traffic pattern
(lady in red orbiting the man with the James Bond eyes).
It's decorations
(why mistletoe outside the bathroom?).
It's sideways glances at newcomers.

I'm the newcomer, the only woman in the room with bourbon and water, cowboy boots,
and a nose bling instead of a wine spritzer.
James-Bond-Eyes has a smear of red lipstick directly beneath his earlobe,
and there's too much water in my drink.

If I shift my weight softly and carefully to the left,
my sleeve brushes yours, and just like in the night,
you reach for me while still carrying on your eye-crinkled smiling conversation
with the three men who are looking at you as if you are a hero.

The door opens,
letting in a blast of the snow-laden air and street sounds.
My heart flips over toward the wind
while my hand snags yours like the hook on a bur.

Chindi Song

for Ivan Brown

He served in the Gulf War,
A simple man, but smart,
With music as his rhythm
And rodeo in his heart.

His Navajo Bear Clan cousins
Pay up to ride 'em wild,
While in the night he hears the chindi
And believes just like a child.

I went to where he heard them,
Those witches that defy
Our modern explanations,
And in the dark I heard them cry.

Witness the witches, witness the night,
Bring on the mystery, bring on the flight.
Witness the chindi that cries before dawn,
We need the darkness, we need his song.

Daylight holds the bear track,
Eagle high above the rocks,
But Venus sings of blackness
And her yodel is the fox.

So lie very still and listen,
Let spooky rock your world.
Hope you hear the chindi
Sing magic from the swirl.

Witness the witches, witness the night,
Bring on the mystery, bring on the flight.
Witness the chindi that cries before dawn,
We need the darkness, we need his song.

His Navajo Bear Clan cousins
Pay up to ride 'em wild,
While in the night he hears the chindi
And believes just like a child.

Falling in Love

I'm falling in love
and it's nothing like the movies.

I'm falling in love with hot coffee mornings
and cold whiskey evenings
and all the long hours in between.

I'm falling in love with a little bay mare
who is just as willing at dusk
as she was at dawn.

I'm falling in love with cast iron
and merino wool and acorns,
with a leftover slice of bacon
tucked inside a tortilla
at two in the afternoon
and we're still twelve miles from camp.

I'm falling in love with that kerosene lantern
in the old cabin. You know the one.

With the Gila monster and his half-smile,
with granite cliffs etched in a language
even I can learn to speak.
The figures point the way.

I'm falling in love
with Willie Matthews's sunset skies
and a John Dofflemyer poem.

With kittens in the hay and eggs in the nest
and the weight of a burlap nosebag.
The patient horses look like veiled women.

I'm falling in love with branding smoke
and an easy sort
and the first long trot of the year.

With winter solstice and spring snow,
summer monsoon and autumn glow.

I'm falling in love and who needs the movies.

The Harder I Work, the Luckier I Get

You are so lucky!
Social media comments,
on my page
over and over again.

You are so lucky!
So lucky
to live where you live,
do what you do,
perhaps even love who you love.
But is love ever lucky?
Last night it felt like work as we tried to say it right.

They say diligence is the mother of luck,
but that won't get pizza delivered way out here,
no matter what time we ride in.

You are so lucky! But I don't feel lucky. I feel tired.
Rode the biggest horse today,
sixteen hands and shaped like a barrel.
My saddle is heavy when lifted up over my head
and now my stirrup is at chin level.

I don't feel lucky.
I feel crusted over with sweat and dirt
after four nights in camp,

sleeping on the ground—
cleaner, I suppose,
than an airport.
My nearest shower is three days out.
Leaning against the wall,
washing my hair with one hand.

I don't feel lucky.
I feel I'm earning my paycheck
one day at a time,
helping to grow food on untillable soil.
Where is the luck in that?

Webster defines luck as
success or failure apparently brought by chance
rather than through one's own actions,

—and I worked hard to get here.

Livin' the dream,
only dreamin' didn't get me here.
Sweat and effort and miles and try,
sacrifice and grit and determination,
paying attention and desire,
wet saddle blankets got me here.

I'm not just taking up a horse,
following him around, looking cute.
Check the box on the application
for last week's blackened fingernails,

the knowledge of how to get up out of Brockmonte Canyon,
and the skill to help lay that cow down
when she has a horn growing into her head . . .
It is brain surgery, baby.

You are so lucky . . .
Tell that to the bull
who just got away,
when I stopped wearing out my horse
in these rocks.
Opted instead for
the six head of mama cows walking nicely up the trail.
I always say the fastest thing in these mountains is a bear,
but today, I am wrong.
Today the fastest thing in these mountains is
three quarters of a ton
when he decides to leave.

You are so lucky!
Well, I guess I am lucky,
posting my pretty pictures and all,
but I still don't have health insurance
and a peasant is still unrepresented when a vote is called
on the floor of the house or the senate
and my freedom to choose is gone
when no one knows that we still exist.

But I suppose I am free to live or die
without insurance or drug company attachments.
Wait, not free. This year it cost us $600 for the privilege.

Please don't get sick.

By lucky, you mean
I am free to ride off into the sunset,
only by the time the sun sets
I am too tired to ride.
I stumble when I pull that sweat-soaked saddle
from the back of that too-tall mount
and he swings his head around just in time
to clock me on the cheekbone.

Living the dream . . .

I want to stand down, sit down, lie down,
let the woodsmoke blow over me,
cleanse me of ones and zeros and who cares about that bull?

But first
we must build that fire
and pull a meal together
and some of the food in the cooler is starting to smell funny.
No ice for the bruise on my cheek.

By sunset there is no way we want to saddle up
and ride off down the canyon singing our pretty songs.

But the canyon will be here in the morning,
as will the bachelor group of bucks silhouetted on the dam,
and the tired coyote who comes to drink;
we'll sleep to his song.
And the baby calves will buck and play while their mothers eat hay
and there will be coffee.

So, come on . . . roll out of that bed.
Make sure you have your hand saw and your fencing pliers,
and enough tie strings,
a good pair of work gloves,
And a wool stocking cap
for when we hang our cowboy hats in the tree.
We'll gather a stash of oak and cedar and,
if we're lucky,
some walnut . . .
Smells so sweet as it burns.

We'll squat beside that old blue pot . . .

Tin cups on cold mornings.

Aren't we lucky?
Now, let's get to work.

Mud

Give me mud,
heavy black fragrant,
goldfish harbor at the bottom of the trough.

Give me cows,
bawling cumbersome social,
daughters and sons and families of cows.

Give me light,
flickering non-electric intimate,
creating a circle of us.

Give me solitude,
days of books and pages and truths,
when the story is the thing.

Give me weather,
storm and wind and brighthot
on unprotected skin.

Give me simple,
and wet,
and real.

Keep your diamonds,
your malls,
your exhaust fumes,
your busy-ness,
your prescriptions,
your clean.

Give me mud,
heavy black fragrant,
dragonfly harbor at the bottom of the trough.

Temple Grandin for President

Temple Grandin for President,
Peace on earth, good will toward men.
If we include women and cows and tree frogs,
The rest of the world will say amen.

You've been hollering and slapping your chaps all morning,
And your horse is plumb sweated through.
I can see you must be a very good hand,
By all the crashing through the bushes you do.

But it might be easier on these critters,
If you'd stop being punchier-than-thou.
If you learned to think less like a cowboy,
And started thinking a bit more like a cow.

That little red heifer with the wide flight zone,
If you'll rein up out of that spot,
You won't have to put her back so much
And your horse won't get lathered and hot.

And that black cow with drooped horns,
The one that keeps squirting out to the side?
And you put her back time and again
Saying she's a dumb broad trying to hide?

Well, see that's her newborn baby,
And pretty much all she cares about.
She's just doing her job to protect him
From all your slaps and your shouts.

I've come to appreciate that the very best hands
Aren't those making the loudest noise.
Just like I don't believe that happiness comes
From buying the biggest toys.

And I don't care how sweaty your horse is,
But I do care that you are thoughtful and kind.
Because often the one who is doing the best job
Uses less of his brawn and more of his mind.

The boss out here likes cows moving quiet.
He treats these animals as important and smart.
He doesn't think they are stupid or mean,
And he works them with kindness and heart.

So when I saddle up to go work for him,
And we get these girls lined out on a drive,
I move my mount and not my mouth,
While I'm earning my seventy-five.

If we respect women and cows and tree frogs,
The whole world can say amen.
Temple Grandin for President,
Peace on earth, good will toward men.

Things Worth Writing a Poem About

It's the cowboy riding two hours
to the top of Elbow Spring,
for that last little group of cows,
but turning, he rides home again,
leaving them behind,
while in juniper shade
the goat-horned heifer
licks her first calf.
He'll return when the time is right.

It's yellow toadstools two days after the rain,
and rock echeveria when it blooms.

It's this phone call:
Mr. Clark? It's Travis.
About tomorrow . . .
Oh, she's fine. Biggr'n a house,
but we have two weeks yet.
No, sir, I don't need to stay home.
It's just that when I went
to hook up my trailer tonight,
well, see, there's a bird nest in the nose,
and I'd just pull it out,
but the eggs have already hatched,
and well, I was just wondering,
could I maybe borrow a horse?

It's riding so long
you aren't hungry anymore,
hearing a zone-tail above the branding pen,
a fox's mating call at dawn,
a bull screaming for girls in the night.

It's the boss who hangs up the phone,
smiling,
knowing he made the right choice
when he hired that kid.

It's my Pa Pa,
at 90,
holding a great-grandson on his knee,
after bath time,
running life-scarred hands over
tender toddler skin,
looking up at his granddaughter to say,
My, he has good hide.

It's knowing
where the bull snake lives,
and that these cows know better than I do
how to get down off this slope.

It's knowing that the bat has sex in the fall,
but doesn't get pregnant 'til spring,
when the time is right.

Charlie's Song

He was not a very old man
Though some days that time seemed close.
He was not always a good man
But he sure tried harder than most.

He had a job he'd come to like
For a man that he respected
And his wife sure liked that house.
But life tends to bring the unexpected.

For lately he'd been thinking
About his rowdy eldest son,
And the potential for serious trouble
If he stayed on the path that he'd begun.

Hanging with a rough crowd
Running hard, playing wild,
And he pondered how to help this boy,
Not quite man, and not quite child.

The cowboy went to his boss
With a question in his heart.
"If I was ever to quit you
Would you give my son a place to start?"

"Why, shore! It'd be a pleasure
To hire a young man with you as dad!"
"Then I quit," said his top hand,
And the boss just could not be mad.

So the cowboy and his wife
Moved a little off down the road
And as promised, his oldest boy moved in,
To straddle the horses Dad once rode.

It's been ten years and since
His father's boots he's filled.
He's solid, smart, and reliable,
Married a sweet girl and is strong-willed.

This song does not have
A catchy hook to sink in.
It's just a love song of fathers
For their sons becoming men.

I saw the old cowboy
In the coffee shop today,
Asked after his boy and
Here's what he had to say:

"I don't know very much
And I wasn't a very good dad,
But I guess I gave my son,
The best job I ever had."

Sad Houses

She made sad houses smile. – Vess Quinlan

The previous cowboy had a pig in the house,
mud marks at knee-level, urine-soaked shag carpet.
I had a two-year old.
Bought cheap white paint. $7/gal.
Tried to clean the carpets.
Couldn't afford a shampoo machine. $70/day. 45 miles to town.
It was July. 105 in the Texas Croton River cedar breaks.
No grass in the camp house yard.
A pack rat under the bathtub, chewing through.
Gyp water from the well, drinking water from a deep cistern, lifted to daylight in a bucket,
antique pulley holding the rope.
The baby played in the water hose.
I stepped on a nail that drove up through the sole of my shoe and into the sole of my foot.
I sat on the stoop and cried.

Nameoflove

The sky is
orangepinkgold
as he walks from the barn;
bestbeerintheworld
in his hand;
Tired horse rolls in the sand.
The house is dark and quiet.
In the kitchen,
he remembers.
Damnittohell.
She is waiting for him,
socialevent
and he is
fuckinlate,
tiredasallgetout,
doesn't mean a
hillabeans
to him,
damnittohell.
Twenty minutes later,
hair wet,
boots still muddy,
roars down the driveway,
halfdrunkbeer
resting
on the toilet tank.

Lightening Up

Standing witness to what?
Blank verse, blank sky, blank days.
Cows chew hay
dropped behind honking horn
that cut the air before 6 a.m.

Doors slamming, water running, bacon frying.
Sipping delayed coffee
we retreat into silence and words—
incendiary and placid both—
until we retreat again with minds alight,
to horse sweat and heavy decisions.

That old broad, does she stay or does she go?
Jesus, I wish it'd rain . . .
Rather go too far, ship too many, cut too deep . . .
Maybe that hard-to-handle bull
and those scrubby little heifers . . .

Not that one, though.
Looks just like her mom.
You know the one I mean—
wide horns, a little white on her bag?
We put her through last month,

black baby at her side, too tiny to brand.
She's still spittin' 'em out—
Gotta be fifteen. Good little cow . . .
And her daughter's the spittin' image.

But—I did say I was gonna lighten up.

Sorting in bright baked pens,
gooseneck gates rattle loudly in the heat.
We've memorized that blank sky—
notice the cottonball cloud when it puffs—
like a changed word in our familiar song.

We look away.

In matters of hope and heart
we long for the low-hanging fruit.
Fulfillment before fatigue sets in.
Too tired to eat or make love or recoup our losses.

The afternoon storm cools, soothes, cleanses.
It wasn't much—but it was a start.
Told tired leaves and dusty roots
to hang on a little longer.
Tomorrow's storm brews
bigger and fatter than its parent.
Moisture breeds moisture,
is what the old men say.

Eating after dark,
only because it is so far to the sale barn.
Returning empty,
then chores. Always chores.

Damp air in the desert
smells different than other airs in the world.
Forks on tin plates.
Ice in amber glasses.

I bear witness as he looks up.

I wish I'd-a kept that heifer.

His Time of Day

The old cow moves and stretches her bones
from her place in the cedar shade.
She calls to her calf, drawing him close,
teaching him not to be afraid.

The man and his horse have just arrived
with his smells and his sounds and his woo.
She sniffs the wind for the hint of hay.
He is making a pasture move.

The red cow turns, walks up the dim trail
with four more of her closest friends.
Their calves are all about the same age,
and possibly, distantly kin.

Years past her ears would have dripped with dogs
and his horse would have foamed with sweat.
Today they all walk in a quiet line,
to join more on the salt ground, he bets.

He values now drives gentle and slow.
The man has been changing his ways.
Autumn's begun informing his song,
commencing his legacy phase.

Someday he'll turn this place over and be
accountable for what he's done.
He likes to see the land bountiful,
with things growing and creeks that run.

The old cow ambles sagely and wise,
her steer trotting close by her side.
She'll bawl for three days when he goes away,
but in her belly, a new one rides.

A slight soft smile creases his face
as the water lot gate grows near.
That red broad in the lead, damn she's old.
For sure he should ship her this year.

But she keeps on bringing 'em to him,
healthy calves, fat, shiny and slick.
He always finds her in the roughest parts
where the best feed is strong and thick.

She's always at the head of her group.
Without struggle or chase leads 'em in.
Now at the tank, she bawls his way,
with water dripping from her chin.

He closes the wire gate as he thinks;
does a quick tally in his mind.
He's shipped several old cows this fall,
and now there's room to keep her kind.

She'll show the young ones how best to move
in the boulders piled high on this place,
and what to eat when it is not so good,
and where the hidden water stays.

Gentle and calm, but knows how to fight
with sharp horns and slinging snot.
The scent of coyote, lion or bear
brings memories of those past battles fought.

But kind eyes rest between her wide horns
that are wrinkled and grooved now thin.
He tosses out flakes of alfalfa hay
as she brings that big steer right on in.

Shaky truth he was fed in his youth:
The country makes them wild, doncha know.
Thick brush and rocks and steep canyon walls
are not like those flats down below.

That way of thinking has now grown old.
He's had years to look at it close.
When cows run off or the creek bank's bare,
he examines his own self most.

And now he stands and watches his girls
as they chew their way through the hay.
Cuts the strings on one more bale because
he can, and this is his time of day.

Diné

The banners of noise wave around my head and my toes dig down into the soles of my shoes until I slip off the impediments—the shoes impede my grounding. Now I am surreptitiously barefoot.

The roused rabble rarely sings—it must shout to be legitimate and it waves symbols of its platform at the camera lens—

MY guns

　　　MY flag

　　MY holy book—

Though there is some confusion about all three. Which book exactly? Which translation? And how exactly is God involved? Surely He is on the side of manifest destiny, but that can't be my heritage. What about the history books?

And which flag, exactly, are they waving while they ask for the dirt and soil and trees and magpies and rivers to be returned to the state(s)?

　　　Utah?

Oregon?　　　Nevada?

　　　　　　Wyoming?

Stars and stripes forever, of course. But what of the 3-letter agencies whose paychecks come from those stars? Fuck 'em! Oh, and Texas already has her land. Always has. It is so confusing.

The only thing they all agree on is guns. Our right to speak and shoot freely.

My toes and the strong pads of my feet dig down until I am knee-deep in the real world, the dirt, the land, the soil, the earthworms. The un-ownable thing being fought for and it doesn't even know it. I wade away from the rabble. I would change my name to Paiute or Crow or Sioux. But they won't have me.

My European genes hide inside my country girl skin and tonight I am the moon's godchild. I long for an indigenous name.

　　　Diné.

Hearts at Half-Mast

July 3, 2013, after the death of nineteen Granite Mountain Hotshots

I will not process this on facebook,
or twitter,
or inciweb where the fire map is an amoeba
eating things.
They were not young men.
They were men:
husbands, fathers, fiancés, sons, friends,
with beards or not . . .
they were human beings doing a job,
a hard job, a paid job,
and they sharpened their chainsaws with files.
I will not process this on the telephone
or standing at a candlelit vigil on the square downtown,
Whiskey Row on one side, flags flying low.
When they call for a moment of silence,
I scream with closed throat for more than a moment.
We ride off from the plugged-in world
for the low country
where there are no thermometers and it is hard to sleep
until the 4 a.m. breeze comes through the open window.
The cows come to the #1 alfalfa
with calves at their sides.
I write in a journal beside a tepid cup of cow camp coffee.

We can smell the smoke of those charred men
from here.
None of them were my son,
but I call my son to say,
Hey, you . . . Mama loves you.
What I want to say is
don't die,
don't ever die,
don't hurt,
don't drive,
don't come off your horse,
don't take your deep voice from me.
Don't bump your head.
Mama can't stand it.

Time's Awastin'

Life's too short
to pass up
raw oysters
shrimp cocktail
(lemon wedges,
horseradish, vinegar, cocktail sauce,
and beer).

Life's too short
to live without
moans,
cravings,
hope, coffee,
evening glow on the rocks.
Be still.

Life's too short
to pat someone on the head
and the ass
four times a day
so he feels like a man.

Life's too short
to worry about
paperwork,
finish a book I don't like,
wear uncomfortable clothing,
stay inside
when the rain falls.

Life's too short
to lock Aphrodite
in the basement,
chains made of panty hose
and hair ribbon,
handfeed others with ideas,
back into every parking space
for a quick getaway.

Life's too short
to cut a heart-shaped escape hatch
into every love,
to use exactly the right words,
every time,
to leave an oyster
un-eaten.

Fall Works Poem

I am riding to camp in the evening,
The sun resting low in the day.
The date marks the start of the season
When the wind gets cool, starts to play.

These horses are shiny and soft,
With bellies full of monsoon grass.
I wish they'd save their energy,
But these fool notions will soon pass.

You're coming behind in the old brown truck
With food and our camp and our gear,
Pulling that rattle-y green trailer
Full of alfalfa so rich and so dear.

We don't ride with a big crew on this outfit.
It's just me and you most of the time.
But we're lovers, so it suits us,
And the work's getting done just fine.

This little bay mare is full of herself,
Kicking at the horse dragging behind.
There's a big job ahead, little sister.
Better settle into a pace you like.

We've reached the creek and the clover is high.
These ponies are scenting a bear.
Maybe the one whose tracks we've been seeing
and I wonder if he'll winter 'round here.

I'm sure looking forward to cow works this fall,
To moving these girls down the way.
To long slow drives with gentle cows
And a toddy at the end of the day.

I'm climbing the hill, almost to camp,
A place of water and work and real.
I'll hobble these mares and wait for you
To build a fire, pour a drink, make a meal.

For a few days we'll gather into this trap,
Drink coffee from that old blue pot,
Strip saddles from the backs of sweating mounts,
And talk about each cow we got.

I'm not sure which stars burn above,
But I bet I'll know by dawn.
I'll lie in our bed with their swing overhead
And me, held snug in your arms.

Tomorrow we start this cow and bull hunt.
It's catch and release every year.
But you couldn't pay me to stay at home
When most of what I love is out here.

Snowed in with Tulips

Everything electric is silent
 since the first morning
 when the wind woke
 to find color and sound
  buried
 and heaved aside the barriers . . .
  broke the blanket—
 and the poles,
  we guess.
The recording says they are aware of the problem.
  Thank you for your call.

It's all about calories.
We swim in dim space
 swaddled
 by a close heavy sky—
 backed
 by roar of yellow fire.
We turn from one to the other—
 pressed.
Forays into the gray with
 grains and flakes
for horses and LGBs
 (misnomer for scarlet, ebony, russet, azure, gold).
We stand and stare at middle storm—
 forced bulbs in a pot: red, white, and green.

41

Sweetly Singing

The alarm sings at 4 a.m.
Ours is a work song—
   a song of doing, with hands and hearts—
      a heartbeat song.
It is an I-N-G song—
   a song of rising, going, growing,
        moving, mounting, being there
where the work is always waiting.

Ours is a living song,
   a defining song, a refining song—
         trial by fire—
a *some days are hard* in four/four time song.
It is a cycle song, a season song,
a never-ending circle song—
        with weather. And death.

Ours is a sweet singing,
a lowing, a keening, a coyote howling in the canyon,
     a falling rain and deepgurgle creek song.
We always sing of water.

Ours is a song of fire and wind,
   wood and plants,
stone and that ancient dance—

a song of trying again
                        and love
            and lists.
Don't forget to stop at the feed store.

Ours is a walking song—
        allegretto upon the trail,
                a single file dust song—
a bawling for babies melody—
        bass notes of bellowing bull telling the whole world that
we are on our way.

Yes, sweetly singing, we are on our way.

Drunk

I get drunk on the smell of the dark places in the creek.

I get drunk on the idea that . . . well, on ideas.

I get drunk on frog song and lupine blue and sego lilies and horse sweat.

I get drunk on any moon, on the sound of a solitary quail at dawn,
on the white foam around a baby calf's lips
and the lowing of his mother when he strays too far.

I get drunk at 5 a.m. when I awaken to see Orion directly overhead.

I get drunk on long, hot, hour-slog days and cooking out of doors.

I stagger.

lifted from night waves

She wanted to be a jellyfish,
      pulsing gently,
a beacon of calm for all who saw her.
Instead,
          she was fireworks in the desert
                   —the Baptist ladies' group standing around
        with buckets of water,
waiting to put out her flames.

Accounting

Balance the column left,
balance the column right.
Black is the goal,
abundant black
to put back
to make more black.
Keep the red
from creeping in,
keep the blood from rising,
staining the page with evidence;
more going out
than is coming in,
so drink more water
to make more blood,
stem the flow,
change it back to black.

Invest,
increase,
scheme, plan,
throw ideas into ink,
looking good on the back of the envelope.
Hope they go ka-ching.
Make sure the deposit
is more than the debit;

sell more than you buy;
hold tight to the promise
of tomorrow's escalation,
tomorrow's profit,
tomorrow's hope
of laying down the crosses
we carry.

But if red is bad
and black is good
and increase is positive
and decrease is negative
and the question is always
do we buy and hold
or gamble our way to more,
then why are strawberries the sweetest,
and why do sunrises bleed,
and why do her bitten lips
make you want to suck them clean?
Why then do you
spend your energy,
spend your creamy essence
down into her darkness
until the turgid member is loose and empty,
and why do you love the sure thing

that is her smile,
heart's gamble already played
and won
and the chips stacked on her side of the bed?

Balance the column left
with bills and worry
and the check is in the mail;
balance the column right
with an eagle,
woodsmoke,
old books,
grandfathering in a clause that allows you
to use all the hot water in the tank,
ignore the rising sun
for a moment we'll never draw against;
fingering the guitar,
each note is free,
black and red together
more abundance and flow
than cash and goal.

Something Sacred This Way Comes

Shout your opinions loudly.
Make your certain positions known.
Never utter "I'm not sure."
Keep staring at your glowing phone.

The fox kits playing in the sycamore shade snap at gnats rising from the pool. They do not know the word stagnant and they do not know words. The hum of summer means food and big and play and mother.

Strident of voice and platform,
Of clan and chapter and team,
You know where you stand, and they will too,
When you share the perfect meme.

The elk strides alone across a mesa as monsoon clouds build and boil and the air changes and the light changes and his back foot is long, narrow, pointed. The hawk joins the sky to swoop amid the currents and add his voice to the thunder.

Of course you know the rights and the laws
And what our forefathers said.
The wise men through the ages weigh in.
We'll quote them and stand on their heads.

The worm does his work on the decaying log and he is not better or worse or less or more than the elegant lion who purrs more loudly than she screams, and pads softly over boulders, and leaves scat at the base of the twisted tree that rises from the edge of the cliff.

Scroll on the screen with swipe and mouse.
Comment, like, unfriend, and follow.
Defend and applaud and chase your tail,
Win your battles and ignore the hollows.

The drying up pools are lusty with life but there is no marrying or giving in marriage or need. The crawdad and the tadpole do not know that they are dying, gasping, close to the end unless the rains really do come to freshen the warm brackish water in the veins of the desert.

Stick close to those who think like you.
Don't give quarter to the other side.
Love those answers that go down smooth,
For we know questions have no pride.

The lonely bear swims in the still water of a shaded spring and sniffs out the fat white grub who tills the soil, in one end and out the other. A saguaro with six arms stands in these rocks longer than there have been white streaks across the sky.

And when you tire of the rhetoric,
Click on "view my cart,"
Indulge in retail therapy.
Let merchandise fill your heart.

The wild is singing a simple song in seven shades of complicated. It sings of lost and loss and light and lissome wind. It moans of dark and dripping and dank and draining and devils in the night.

Something sacred this way comes.

Sunday Morning Dawning

Sunday morning dawning, pale light October, you murmur in my ear. And before the song comes the sounds of an election year. But under the blankets, calming, we remember the ancient caves. When we loved. When we hated. Love won, you know. And we were saved. We made music. We made war. We made beauty. We had more. When we sang. When we baked cakes and shared with those who did not celebrate the same ways and days. Our children played together beneath the laurel trees. We sweated and worked and planted and danced under the same moon. Mothers will always say *eat your breakfast.* And someone will always try to stir us up, one against the other, with false graphics, rhetoric. And the wise will say *I don't know the answers, but please sit by my fire and together we will cure the cancers of misunderstanding.* And one coffee bean will always escape the grinding blades, shiny and whole amidst the grounds. And lovers will make love before dawn. And you will make me laugh. And someone will say *put whiskey on the shopping list.* And the perfect orange feather by the cow-shat water hole in the creek will make perfect sense.

And the poets will try to write it all down.

Plundered

We have bleached everything—
Our sugar, our salt, our flour, her hair.
We've cut away everything—
Our forests, our jungles, our beaches, the soft silk from under her arms.
Pluck, eliminate, alter, and shave.
Dye and slash and mine and pave.
We cut away the mountain slope
And stuffed bags of saline under her fragile skin—
Call it a boob job . . . to make her more boob-tiful—
I hope they don't leak like the rubber-lined sludge ponds in the oil field.
No big deal. It is only desert.
Spill garbage into our seas, a fresh crunchy coating for the fish and birds and
                    gasping playful otters—
Bunch the beeves into shitty pens. Call them food. You'll feel better.
You are what you eat.
Bullets whiz over our heads, but we don't look up.
They'll tell us about it on the news.
Don't let anyone take your guns.
No one has come yet, but I am watching.
Manicure and pedicure and coiffure and tan,
Whisper to her sweetly that
the word *environmentalist* is wrong.
Also *feminist*.
Airbrush and photoshop, a little here, a little there. Fake is the new real.

Spray her with pesticides and herbicides—Where are all the bees?
Oh, well, who needs honey? I use bleached and processed,
                    snow white sugar.
She slept a long time, you know.
Brush your teeth with plastic beads and then eat a teaspoonful in your tilapia.
Nature brings things full circle, a righteous recipe.
Rub ointment made in a laboratory into the fine lines that life brought you.
We can trust the men in white coats.
Men in white coats?
Oh. You are one of those women.
Why, yes. Yes, I am.

One In A Million

A million demands over digital feed,
A million decisions to make this week,
A million grains of sand at my feet,
A million hooks to snag my attention,
One is caught in the soft flesh of my cheek.

A million strands of DNA,
A million springtime newborns play,
A million hosts, a million ghosts,
Millions of leaves on a million trees,
And isn't that enough?

A million songs sung over intercoms,
Marking three minute intervals inside walls where there is no dawn.
A million songs from a handful of frogs,
And a hawk comes to drink from the vibrating pool.
She's one in a million, baby.

A few million blades of grass
Rising from the trick tank of rocky slope and we say
Man, it looks good on this mountain.
I post a triumphant photo as if I germinated a million seeds,
And someone comments, *What do the cows eat in that country?*
A dose of humble from the rumble of just how far we have come from dirt.

Come see the wind, hold the sun, hear the rock,
Taste the flight of the swallowtail from bush to bush, smell the clover dampness.
Come to the creek, stand beside me on that million song mountain.

A million lights burn and shine
Edison's pollution and beyond his time,
But they say even he couldn't measure or count the billions of explosions
And delayed shinings surrounding our flat-footed existence.
I should have just said stars.

A million hens lay a million eggs every afternoon.
Scrambled, poached, boiled, over-easy.
Give them 21 days and a warm broody fierceness,
To make a million miracles peeping.

A million dollars isn't that many dollars anymore
So I'll choose a million moments with my feet on this big rock,
Her orbit making me a little seasick.

Millions of people looking for love
And two million have found it.
A million couples murmuring a million mundanities a month.

A million motors, a million buildings,
More buildings than people who need shelter from millions of raindrops falling.
Who doesn't need to get a little wet?
I know my face is dirty.

The Buddhists offer torma, a little cake,
A physical offering to the ghosts, to the negative aspects of self.
I'll take a million, please.

A million days divided by 365 equals 2739, almost 40,
That's a lot of years, a lot of spins, a lot of sighs, a lot of tries—
Tomorrow is a brand-new day.

A million breaths or heartbeats don't add up to much,
But a million cups of coffee or invitations to laugh or dance or cry,
Those might cause us to hold hands at the end,
Allowing a million of my cells to mingle with a million of yours.

Building Fires

I've pulled up,
let everyone ride ahead of me in the jig line.

I came here thinking I was tough,
that I could learn to do almost anything.

Three days later I lay defeated on cold ground
beneath sky too big,
beside rocks too hard
and brush too thick
and slopes too steep
and shouted orders coming too fast and too complicated.
—I know nothing.

Tomorrow, I'll cinch up all wrong.

After only five or six years of self-doubt and uncertainty,
I sit by the fire and almost know the right questions to ask,
make a few drives almost in the right place.

Block a trail without being told.
Almost.
The shouter stops mid-shout when he sees I am already there.

Throw my loop in the dirt twice in a pen of fifteen calves.
Start asking a different set of questions.

But there are spurs on my feet
and a sweated hat on my head
and my saddle is no longer new.
I should oil it on a Sunday afternoon.

Five or six miles away, cobwebs sully the corners
and laundry piles beside my unmade bed
because this morning
I crawled out from under *this* canvas
to start *this* dawn fire
while horses chewed their way through hay and grain.

I am a key player in the day's game.
Flank up after we shove 'em through the gate,
spend the whole morning tucking cows back in—
walk along, girls, walk along.

The sky spreads from edge to edge doing a true west stretch.

We do the horseback dance,
sorting the herd,
but I'm still smoothing out the turns and steps and bends.
Call my horse Twinkletoes,
and laugh when we are done.

Slide off to help kindle a different fire,
pull my cinch extra tight—
there are some big longears in this bunch.
A disgruntled Twinkletoes—
she thought I said we were done.

I've learned not to count the calves
with complete ears and pristine hide
because it takes as long as it takes.
We work our way through
and I'm finally at a place where I can
joke with the crew,
built loop resting in my right hand.
One of the few times in my life when I've felt graceful,
when I've found grace.

I know the drive to Mud Spring—
could do it in my sleep.
Or the rain.
Or the almost dark.
Hold 'em up on water
before trotting back to camp for two cool beers,
my shirt damp with sweat,
salt from my lips on the rim of the can,
sun boiling the evening clouds.

Throw hay to the shippers
and water the horses
and look at the crack in Bonnie's hoof.

Break up some wood,
tiny twigs and tree bark, blow hard—
I'm building another fire.

Beef from the cooler
and scent of smoke
while patties sizzle—

no more hair on my knuckles,
the chuckles of cooking over wood.

Camp buttoned up for the night
and our bed rolled on the ground.
I stand in the early dark, not ready to lie down.

The sky is still too big,
the rocks are still too hard,
the brush is still too thick,
the slopes still rise above, neverending.

None of that has changed.

But there is a fire overhead that I didn't build
and I'm carrying some of my own.

It burns hot behind my eyes

. . . to write about love

What would I write if I were
to write about love?
Perhaps I would write of the very moment of waking
when I am filled with adoration or disgust.
Most often adoration—
so much more often that the disgust
does not bear mentioning
other than to point out this is real love,
the kind that stays
and waits for the adoration to catch up later
over coffee.
Perhaps I would write about
washing my hair in the creek
by Alkali Spring
while I wait with three horses.
About washing my hair in the creek
and drying it in the sun
and wishing I could show you that I am that kind of girl—
the kind who goes ten days without
shower or power
but washes her hair in the creek
while she waits for you.
Of course, there was no soap.

If I were to write about love
I'd have to mention that no one has ever loved me
that way—
the obsessed, you are my only love, never let you go,
please don't leave me, buy you diamonds,
wrap you in cotton wool
kind of way.
Well, maybe there were a couple of guys
but they were stupid young
and never counted.
And of course I'd have to mention
A son—bear strong and perfect flawed.
A daughter—brilliant smart and every thirty days lost.
The bleeding out all I have kind of love.
I must go away now
for my pen is out of ink
and my wings are nailed to the ground.

Tough Enough

Sometimes I just want to be a girl.
I don't want to be so tough . . .
I want to turn and ride to the house,
Say, Hey boys, I've had enough.

Sometimes I want to wear lip gloss
Instead of this mustache made of dirt,
Wear something pretty and slinky and pink
Instead of these chaps and denim shirt.

Sometimes I want to pull up
Instead of going crashing through the brush,
Say, Sorry, honey, I didn't get there in time,
But you know how I hate to rush!

Some days I count the pairs in the pen
And I don't want to head them all.
I don't want to mill in the dust and smoke,
And listen to those babies bawl.

Sometimes I want to sleep in my own bed
Instead of wrapped in canvas and wool,
But to give up this glorious job
I'd be three kinds of a fool.

For it is often through miles and testing
That a girl can find her strong,
And sometimes, the most luminous beauty
Comes from days that are hard and long.

And these cowboy days have taught me well
About some other parts of life,
Like kids and love and trails and logic
And don't ever forget your pocketknife.

The truth is that I like these cows.
I like how they move through the world.
I like to be in the wide outside
And don't care if my hair is curled.

So, tomorrow I will saddle right up
And ride no matter the weather.
I'll pull on my boots, don my hat,
And fill my hands with leather.

I'll look deeper than the dirt and sweat,
Show up to ride all day,
Try to treasure the moments money can't buy,
Count those as the bulk of my pay.

Sometimes I just want to be a girl.
I don't want to be so tough . . .
But as I put these words on the page,
I figure, I'm tough enough.

Smith Canyon Meditation After a Pedicure

Camping out with my pretty toes
and I don't know how to make them
un-pretty
even though tonight
I don't feel pretty or girly,
but strong and wild.
I squat
and my pee hits a rock.
My water splashes onto my pretty toes.
I crabwalk six inches to the left so it only goes
into the sand.

Don't miss these fine novels
by WILLA award-winning author
Amy Hale Auker!

Winter of Beauty

The winter Bride wears diamonds. To those down below, she appears to be sleeping, locked inside a chastity belt of cold. She naps lightly behind the veil of ice and snow, letting it shield her from the sun and throw it back into the sky.

But her chill is only skin deep. Inside her hidden folds and caves and recesses, the heartbeat of her lives and breathes and curls around the seeds of what will be. The winter Bride is pregnant, gestating the future, smiling quietly at the snores of the bears and the mountain lions, allowing all of the fertile places to swell and burgeon with the life that is to come.

The winter Bride is holding a flood in deposit for the sun's withdrawal in spring.

"Amy Hale Auker has found her own voice with which she has created a refreshing style of storytelling. It is obvious she has a broad understanding of the politics and traditions of a ranch. It is also obvious she loves the West. She stays spot on with the cycles, moods and language that have evolved within the ranching community. Her characters have the recognizable traits of folks from the same lifestyle and heritage. I tasted the food and the pain and the cold and the friendships. *Winter of Beauty* will stand the test of time."

~ Waddie Mitchell, co-founder of the National Cowboy Poetry Gathering

Read a FREE chapter or get your copy today!
at www.Pen-L.com/WinterOfBeauty.html

The Story Is the Thing

"Uncle Bill" Morgan knew about love and loss. He had watched over the land and the people at the Benson Ranch for decades. Julia was a free spirit, quirky and fun, trapped in a marriage with hospital corners and traditional expectations. Charlie was trapped as well, but by something more sinister than tradition and, in the end, realized that it is okay to love more. Cody Jack needed more — more of everything that soothed and comforted and numbed — but he stood to lose the only good thing he'd ever known and he would hurt anyone to keep it.

The old cowboy is gone, but he left his story behind. It is a story of love, loss and life lessons, of confession and absolution, a story of poetry and rescue, a story of loneliness and a story of coming together.

And, after all, the story is the thing.

"Amy Hale Auker is a writer with a capital W. You will not pass through this book without being touched by it."
~ Dave Stamey, Cowboy Entertainer

"*The Story Is the Thing* is a real page-turner, and any thoughts I had of 'skimming' it were quickly disabused by the end of the first chapter. Ms. Auker can write and she weaves a tale of love and loss in the big ranch country that grips your attention to the very end. A fine book by a gifted storyteller."
~ Ian Tyson, Musician, Rancher, and Storyteller

"This is a challenging work by a very gutsy, gifted writer with large ambitions. One gets the sense that Ms. Auker is poised to reach beyond that which is so intimately familiar to her—the cowboy West—and break free of all genre labeling. Watch out, here she comes."
~ Kurt Markus, Photographer, Videographer, Screenwriter

"*The Story is the Thing* by Amy Hale Auker is one of the loveliest, most beautifully written, and deeply sensitive books I've read in ages."
~ Helene Benardo, at *Story Circle Book Reviews*

"Chances taken, love lost, lessons learned, life moves on. *The Story Is the Thing* is the third book written by Amy Hale Auker and with each book her writing gets better, her words more lyrical, her story more heart-felt, more poignant. This book is written like a love letter."
~ Maria Norcia Santillanes

&

Thanks for supporting your Western authors!

Photo by Jessica Brandi Lifland

About Amy

Amy Hale Auker writes and rides on a ranch in the Santa Maria Mountains of Arizona. She is the author of two works of creative nonfiction, *Rightful Place,* which won the WILLA Award, and *Ordinary Skin: Essays from Willow Springs,* as well as two novels, *Winter of Beauty* and *The Story Is the Thing.* This is her first collection of poems.

Visit Amy at:
www.amyhaleauker.com

Dear Reader,
If you enjoyed this book enough to review it for Goodreads, B&N, or Amazon.com, I'd appreciate it!
Thanks, Amy

Find more great reads at
Pen-L.com

Made in the USA
Columbia, SC
05 December 2018